M000314254

To: _____

From: _____

Isn't He Beautiful?

Isn't He Beautiful?

A For Better or For Worse® Little Book

Lynn Johnston

Andrews McMeel Publishing

Kansas City

ISBN: 0-7407-1045-1

Library of Congress Catalog Card Number:
00-102166

Poem by Andie Parton

Isn't He Beautiful?

From the time that you know

What your tummy will show

And an army of experts

surrounds you

And you just can't be sure

If you're really mature

To take on this new role that

astounds you

Sure your baby is new

But you're new to him too

So have faith in your own heart

and soul

Sure as stars up above
You'll be falling in love

And the mothering path

will unfold

But sleep deprivation
That awful sensation
In this life will it ever be right?

Body screaming for rest

As you're put to the test

ANY ATTEMPT TO COMMUNICATE WITH ME BEFORE I HAVE HAD AT LEAST ONE CUP OF COFFEE MAY RESULT IN SERIOUS CONSEQUENCES.

Will he ever stay down
through the night?

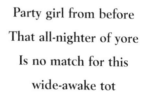

Party girl from before

That all-nighter of yore

Is no match for this

wide-awake tot

Haggard face, ratty hair

Baggy eyes, glassy stare

One night's sleep,
is that asking a lot?

♥

Sure, you're feeling so sore
But your baby wants more
So just air yourself out
and don't hide it

But when he wants to stop

With one full and one not

It's not funny to be so lopsided

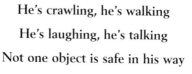

He's crawling, he's walking

He's laughing, he's talking

Not one object is safe in his way

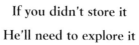

If you didn't store it
He'll need to explore it

Just like you are,

he's busy all day

Potty training is here

He will learn, never fear

He won't leave in a diaper

for college

And you sit by his side

When he "goes" with great pride

Every "trophy" just adds to
his knowledge

Baby snug in your arm
Keeping safe from all harm
This sweet child that you
lovingly kiss

Busy baby at rest

To refuel for what's next

Could an angel be sweeter

than this?

Time goes by fast

And too soon, it's all past

Hold him to you with

all of your might

Put your worries aside

Let your heart be your guide

And your baby can

show you the light.